A DK PUBLISHING BOOK

Project Art Editor *Wendy Bartlet*
Project Editor *Lesley Malkin*
Managing Art Editor *Amanda Lunn*
Senior Managing Editor *Mary-Clare Jerram*
Production Manager *Ruth Charlton*
US Editor *Barbara Minton*

First American edition, 1998
Second American edition, 2006
06 07 08 09 10 9 8 7 6 5 4 3 2 1
Published in the US by DK Publishing, Inc.
375 Hudson Street, New York, New York 10014

A Cataloging-in-Publication record for this book is available from the Library of Congress.

ISBN 0-7566-2260-3

Text film output in Great Britain by R & B Creative Services Ltd
Reproduced in Singapore by Colourscan
Printed and bound in China by Hung Hing Offset Printing Co., Ltd.

Cat's CHRISTMAS

BRUCE FOGLE & MALCOLM HILLIER

London • New York • Munich
Melbourne • Delhi

Grand
entrances

A fine example of Picatso's dramatic entrance

into the art world, this exquisite installation piece

is executed in green moss and red holly berries. An

important work, first displayed at the Christmas

Exhibition, it is signed in pawprints on the reverse

but the artist's signature is difficult to attribute.

A bird
in the paw...

4

A beautifully
executed gift

Indulgence

is the "mot du jour" at Christmas, with the

annual Fish Feast as a high point for all discerning cats. To

ensure tradition is appropriately upheld, a decorative wreath packed with

fish (left) adorns a wall, and guests are served with generous helpings of Fish

Flan. To make 20 servings, arrange 142 fresh fish around the edge of a giant oval

flan dish. Fill the middle of the Christmas Fish Flan with a heap of thinly

sliced and lightly sautéed liver, and strain several cups of best quality

aspic over the top. Chill overnight until set. Remove from

the refrigerator and serve with an optional

garnish of birds' feathers.

Forbidden
fruits

Dangling
baubles of perfection,
reduced to tangled shreds
and shiny shards with the
cheeky swipe of a well-
aimed paw.

Alley

Essential items for the
adventurous alleycat.

WIND-UP MECHANICAL
RAT

•

NAIL FILE TO SHARPEN
CLAWS

•

WIRE CUTTERS FOR
SWIFT ENTRY

•

MOBILE PHONE TO
RALLY THE GANG
FOR A NIGHT
ON THE TOWN

•

POUCH FOR COLLECTING
MICE

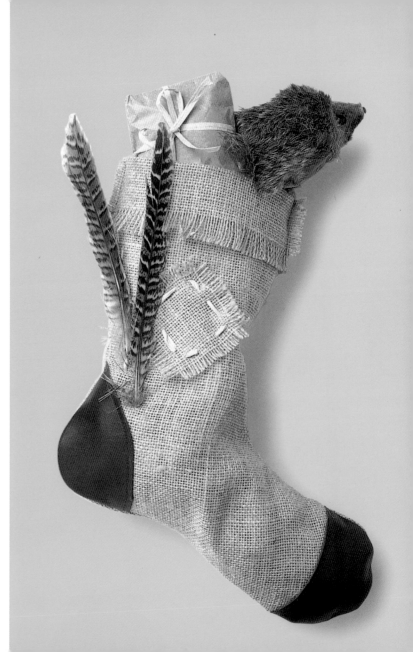

Aristo

Purrfect presents to pamper the aristocat that never ventures outdoors.

NAIL POLISH FOR
CAREFULLY MANICURED
CLAWS

•

CATNIP-SCENTED
HAIRSPRAY

•

LARGE FEATHER-FILLED
VELVET CUSHION

•

SERVING OF THE FINEST
FOIE GRAS

•

MONOGRAMMED BOWL

Completely
crackers

*Amuse all feline friends in the best
of British tradition with five jokes
from the inside of Christmas crackers.*

Q WHAT DO CATS STRIVE FOR?
A *Purrfection.*

Q WHAT DO YOU CALL A CAT
THAT'S JUST EATEN HALF A DUCK?

A *A duck-filled fatty puss.*

•

Q HOW MANY MICE DOES IT TAKE
TO MAKE A MOUSSE?

A *One if it's rich enough.*

Q WHAT HAPPENS IF A MOUSE
RUNS BETWEEN YOUR WHISKERS?

A *You get a mousetache.*

•

Q WHAT'S THE BIGGEST SPECIES
OF MOUSE IN THE WORLD?

A *A hippopotamouse.*

Christmas
menu

APPETIZER
Trio of fresh mice

—◆—

MAIN COURSE
"Poussin de Bresse rôti"
with cocktail sausages
and shrimps, and a
sauce "crème parfumée
aux deux fromages"
with a garnish of freshly
plucked feathers

—◆—

DESSERT
Whipped double cream
and
after-dinner mice

Powder
room

'Tis

the season

to be jolly, so for

a festive touch to the

litter box, paw up some snowy

white litter peaks, and decorate with

fake fir trees. Form an artfully curving path

with natural clay particles, but take care not to pile

the litter too high. Do remember to watch out for the trees!

Seven deadly sins at Christmas...

gluttony

gluttony

gluttony

gluttony

gluttony

lust

gluttony

Kitsch
Christmas

Caught

...in the act

Diary
of destruction

December 24

9.30AM *Taunted the dog from the safety of the garden fence*

10.20PM *Created a crafty diversion and helped myself to the turkey from the kitchen table next door*

December 25

11.30AM *Cunningly opened the refrigerator door and procured the bowl of brandy butter*

1.00PM *Deposited Christmas excesses on the Persian rug*

1.30PM *Redistributed cat litter all around the kitchen*

2.30PM *Gave an Oscar-winning performance protesting that I hadn't been fed*

3.00PM *Failed to resist the temptation of sinking my claws into the presents and shredded the wrappings to pieces*

December 26

7.30AM *Carried off a death-defying acrobatic feat and successfully sent the tree flying across the room*

December 28

10.00AM *Wreaked havoc in the vet's waiting room having offending Christmas-present-shredding-claws clipped*

10.10AM *Dispatched the vet for minor surgery*

" *Peace on earth,*

goodwill to all

dogs ...

for now"

Mega
bytes

Party
paw dips

Invite everyone in for a stylish and glitzy
Christmas cat-tail party. Word of the
devilishly delectable paw dips will quickly
spread and soon there won't be room to
swing a cat!

SALMON SUPREME

Purr-ee 12 mouthfuls of Scottish salmon to a smooth paste. Whisker two catbowls of whipping cream into peaks and mix with the salmon paste.

CATNIP DIP

Claw 10 pawfuls of catnip leaves into shreds. Whisker two catbowls of rich cream into peaks and carefully paw in the shredded catnip leaves.

LIVER MOUSSE

Grind generous pawfuls of liver and mix in one catbowl of sour cream and one catbowl of cream cheese, using several quick flicks of the tail.

Feline
charades

*Is it a book? Is it a film? Is it a play?
Cat thespians emerge at Christmas.
Match the film titles below with this
feline rogue's gallery.*

THE GODFATHER

TWISTER

GREMLINS

FIDDLER ON THE ROOF

GHOST

E.T. THE EXTRA-TERRESTRIAL

Hark!

the can opener

New Year's
resolutions

1 *Pay attention to my owner at all times, not just before a meal.*

2 *Always use the litter box and not the house plants.*

3 *Only scratch designated posts.*

4 *Stay out of territorial disputes with other local cats.*

5 *Treat the vet with compassion.*

6 *Be kind, caring, and considerate.*

7 *Sleep on, not under, the blankets.*

8 *Only regurgitate food and furballs outside.*

9 *Avoid self-indulgence.*

10 *Forget all the above. Be myself!*

Authors' Acknowledgments

Malcolm Hillier and Bruce Fogle would like to thank Stephen Bennington and Jay Musson for making the Christmas stockings on pages 12–13, and Nigel Phillips for constructing the cat flap on page 2 and mouse hole on pages 6–7. Thanks also to Angela Astwood, Dina Dimacopoulu, Mary Bee, and Rodney Engen for all their help and support. Last but not least, thank you to the enigmatic Ocicat twins, Tiger and Roo, for their inspiration.

Publisher's Acknowledgments

DK would especially like to thank photographer Stephen Hayward for his patience, sense of fun, and spontaneous creativity. We also thank Bella Pringle for her editorial work, Helen Trent for sourcing the props on pages 16–17, and Tony and John at The Colour House for retouching the photograph on pages 14–15.

Photography

All still life photography by Stephen Hayward, and all cat photography by Jane Burton, Dave King, and Marc Henrie.